BIRDHOUSES

BIRDHOUSES

Creating a Backyard
Haven for Birds

Margaret MacAvoy, Pat Kite, and Jennifer Markson

BIRDHOUSES

Creating a Backyard Haven for Birds

Margaret MacAvoy,
Pat Kite, and
Jennifer Markson

MetroBooks

MetroBooks

An Imprint of the Michael Friedman Publishing Group, Inc.

Portions of the text for this book were previously published in *The Bird Lover's Garden*.

Library of Congress Cataloging-in-Publication Data available upon request.

ISBN 1-58663-783-5

Editor: Susan Lauzau
Designer: Kirsten Berger
Art Director: Jeff Batzli
Photography Editor: Paquita Bass
Production Manager: Michael Vagnetti

Color separations by Bright Arts Graphics (S) Pte Ltd
Printed in China by Asia Pacific Offset Inc.

10 9 8 7 6 5 4 3 2 1

For bulk purchases and special sales, please contact:
Michael Friedman Publishing Group, Inc.
Attention: Sales Department
230 Fifth Avenue
New York, NY 10001
212/685-6610   FAX 212/685-3916

Visit our website:
www.metrobooks.com

Contents

Fostering Wild Birds

Above: Northern flickers are cavity-nesters who will use a nest box, though they typically excavate holes for their nests in trees, fenceposts, or telephone poles.

Birds bring life to the garden, both literally and metaphorically, adding the important dimension of movement to a world filled with firmly rooted plants. It's a joy to watch them flit from tree to tree, gathering material for their nests or food for their fledglings.

Many of us feel lucky when we look up to see a winged visitor hopping across the lawn or serenading us from a nearby branch, but attracting birds to your yard needn't be a matter of happenstance. There are simple, specific things that you can do to make your backyard a haven for birds, and this book is designed to guide you in choosing effective bird attractors.

While viewing birds is certainly pleasurable, there's an even greater reason to create a safe environment for our feathered friends. An important part of the ecosystem, birds are under increasing threat due to shrinking habitats, disturbed migration

Above: Backyard birders who put up nest boxes have done much to ensure healthy populations of Eastern bluebirds, who are sometimes outcompeted for natural cavities by non-native birds such as European starlings and English sparrows.

routes, deadly pesticides, and other side effects of expanding human civilization. Making your garden a welcoming spot for birds helps assure the continued presence of these wild creatures, strengthening the entire web of life in your neighborhood ecosystem. Families concerned about the environment and interested in doing their part will find bird fostering a fun and rewarding activity that has the added benefit of teaching young children a sense of stewardship of the earth.

This book gives you the practical information you need to turn your own backyard into a bird-friendly zone, with plenty of hints and tips for attracting many different birds. By adding supplemental features—such as birdhouses, baths, and feeders—you can increase the likelihood of attracting all your favorite birds even as you add beautiful ornaments to your garden.

Chapter One

Birdhouse Basics

All too often, homeowners hang up a pretty painted birdhouse, sit back, and wait for the bird family to move in. And all too often, spring turns to summer and autumn turns to winter with no more than the usual number of bird visitors to the garden, none of which show the slightest interest in the Victorian cottage in the sky. Only birds that normally nest in cavities—including bluebirds, chickadees, house wrens, woodpeckers, and many other species—will set up residence in a birdhouse or nest box, and many of these will only choose houses that meet their very particular requirements.

Right: Open grassy areas or flower-filled meadows bordered by dense shrubbery and tall trees provide ideal habitats for many birds. Hanging a functional birdhouse will improve your chances of attracting certain birds.

8

A Home for the Birds

Nest boxes are typically simple, rectangular affairs with the no-nonsense intent of providing homes for nesting pairs. These are simple to make, and are particularly popular with bluebirds. Nesting platforms, which are open on at least one side, are favored by some birds, including robins.

Birdhouses tend to be shaped more like people's houses and are perhaps more ornamental, but good ones have the same straightforward functionality as nest boxes. Both may also be used by birds as winter shelter. Special roosting boxes (which have their holes in the floor) are also available for this purpose. You can purchase ready-made birdhouses and nest boxes from garden suppliers or pet supply stores, or you can make your own.

Unfortunately for the backyard birder, the matter is not as simple as just installing a birdhouse. Different species have exacting requirements, and will reject a house that does not suit their needs precisely. Even more horrifyingly, a bird that unwittingly chooses a house that is not safe may suffer for it—for instance, some plastic or ceramic houses or houses with metal roofs have been known to "cook" young birds once the high heat of summer arrives.

Ideally, birdhouses and nest boxes should be made of wood—remember that this is the material that cavity-nesting birds are accustomed to in nature. Every birdhouse needs several ventilation holes (in addition to the entrance hole) to allow heat to escape and fresh air to circulate. If you've purchased a birdhouse that doesn't feature adequate ventilation, drill ¼-inch (6.5mm) holes yourself. In addition, you'll need several drainage holes in the floor of the house to let rainwater run out.

The size of the entrance hole and the overall dimensions of the birdhouse are among the most important factors in making the dwelling satisfactory to nesting pairs. Each species has its own

Which House for Which Bird?

Species	Floor Dimensions	Depth	Entrance Hole Diameter	Entrance Height from Floor	Height above Ground
Barn owl	10" x 18"	15"–18"	6"	4"	12'–18'
Bluebird (Eastern)	5" x 5"	8"	1½"	6"	5'
Chickadee	4" x 4"	8"–10"	1⅛"	6"–8"	4'–15'
Carolina wren	4" x 4"	6"–8"	1½"	1"–6"	6'–10'
House wren	4" x 4"	8"–10"	1¼"	1"–6"	6'–10'
Northern flicker	7" x 7"	16"–18"	2½"	14"–16"	6'–20'
Screech owl	8" x 8"	12"–15"	3"	9"–12"	10'–30'

preferences, so don't expect to draw a wide variety of birds with the same house. A bird should fill the entrance to its house, that is, the hole should not allow in anything bigger than the bird. The entrance hole need not have a perch below it; these are completely unnecessary for the birds, who fly right to the entrance edge anyway. And perches make the job of predators much easier, as they have something to grip as they attempt their attack on the nest. (See the sidebar Which House for Which Bird? to find out the best dwelling for the birds you want to attract.)

To help young birds crawl up to the entrance hole, the interior wood should be somewhat rough. If you are using finished wood,

Above: The unconventional entrance hole hasn't discouraged this house wren, one of the least fussy cavity-nesters. Wrens will even use a house that hangs from a tree branch; most birds prefer that the house be attached securely to a tree trunk or post.

consider carving horizontal grooves below the entrance hole on the inside of the house. Alternatively, install 1/4-inch (6.5mm) galvanized mesh on the interior wall below the entrance hole.

Never ever paint the inside or the entrance hole of your birdhouse. If you want to paint or stain the outside of the house, be sure to purchase a water-based exterior paint or stain. Wood preservatives are generally ill-advised, but you may be able to find one of a few that the Environmental Protection Agency (EPA) has approved for use with animals and plants: look for Cuprinol wood preservative clear #20 or green #10. Birds are attracted by bright colors, but so are predators. Dark green or brown blend with the environs, and so are less visible to cats, raccoons, and other raiders. If you choose a more decorative scheme, take special precautions to deter predators.

Opposite: Painted a cheerful blue and decked with sprays of pastel flowers, this nest box becomes a lovely garden accent as well as a home for backyard birds. If you plan to decorate your birdhouse, make sure to choose a water-based paint intended for exterior use.

Keeping Birds Safe from Predators

If you have lots of marauding predators in your neighborhood, you may need to take extra precautions to keep them away. Once you've drawn birds to your birdhouse, stay vigilant for cats and squirrels, and chase them away. With any luck, they'll come to learn that the birdhouse is not worth their time and trouble. Keep your family pets indoors (while dogs can't usually catch a healthy bird, they will chase them away) and report strays to your local ASPCA. A predator guard, a small piece of wood with an entrance hole cut into it, will make the entry passage into the house longer, deterring many nest raiders. If you live in an area that is home to tree snakes, you'll also have to watch out for these—plastic mesh encircling the tree trunk will deter the snakes from reaching their goal.

Siting the Birdhouse

Birds feel as strongly about the proper height for their houses as they do about other home matters, so it's important to place the right house at the right height for the species you want to attract (see sidebar on page 12). Five feet (1.5m) seems to be a popular requirement, and is appropriate for such popular backyard birds as chickadees, bluebirds, nuthatches, titmice and wrens. Remember that a healthy dose of experimentation is the key to successfully attracting birds. If, after a few weeks, your house remains unoccupied, try moving it up a bit.

Very few birds will nest in crowded conditions. Typically, the houses must be located

Left: Even a roughly built nest box or birdhouse will do the trick if you put it in the right spot. Bluebirds are among the easiest birds to attract to nest boxes in the backyard, because they like the mix of wooded lots and open spaces that most suburbs provide.

200 or 300 feet (60.9 or 91.4m) apart, depending on the species. This means that the average suburban backyard, which is about ¼ acre (0.1ha), can support only one or two birdhouses. If you are lucky enough to have more land, go ahead and set up more houses. Some birds, most notably martins, will nest in "bird condos," the houses with several living spaces within the same building. This may be a good solution if you want lots of nesting birds but have a small garden.

Note that birds gravitate most to houses situated in the sun. This is not so difficult to arrange if you are planning on affixing the house to a free-standing post, but is considerably

Right: Purple martins prefer their houses to be perched high above an open lawn and, unlike most birds, they don't mind sharing. Anywhere from ten to thirty nesting pairs will settle into one of these multi-roomed houses, though each pair requires its own "apartment."

more tricky if you want to install your house on the trunk of a tree. Observe the tree where you plan to put the birdhouse, and make sure that the front of the house will get at least six hours of sun each day. In addition, the house should be sited so that howling winds and the rains they bring will not squall through the entrance hole. If your yard is subject to prevailing winds, try to locate your house so that the back of the structure is generally to the wind. Whether you are attaching the house to a tree or to a post, be certain to affix it securely, using rust-proof nails. Birds don't like rickety, swaying houses

Opposite: A birdhouse mounted on a free-standing pole can easily be positioned in the sunny situation birds like.

Right: Native Americans were the first to hang hollowed gourds for birds to nest in, and today many people continue the tradition, though some use actual gourds and others have simply adopted the shape. This glazed gourd, inhabited by a house wren, is one such example.

any more than people do. For this reason, they also prefer houses that are mounted to a stable support rather than suspended from branches. Wrens are one of the few species that don't seem to mind a house that hangs.

The Birdhouse Environment

Siting your birdhouse in the preferred surroundings of the bird you are trying to attract will make the birds more comfortable and therefore more likely to use the house. This handy chart shows the favorite environs of some of the birds most likely to nest in backyards.

Forests	Chickadees, nuthatches, titmice
Meadows and fields	Bluebirds
Areas near houses and barns	Swallows, wrens
Edge of pond or river	Purple martins, flycatchers

Care and Maintenance

Make sure to clean your birdhouses and nest boxes out after each nesting, as some birds won't choose an untidy box. Once you've removed old nesting material, dust the interior of the house with 1 percent rotenone powder (an organic pesticide), which will kill any parasites that might have infested the house.

Also check birdhouses periodically if they are not in use to be sure that debris has not gathered and to confirm that unwelcome residents, such as mice or wasps, have not invaded. If wasps or bees prove to be repeat tenants, rub bar soap inside the roof of the birdhouse to deter them.

Each year, check that the wood and the hardware of the birdhouse are in good condition. Sand and repaint wood if paint is peeling and replace screws, hooks, or latches that have rusted or appear loose.

Right: Eastern bluebirds typically raise two broods each year, laying the eggs sometime between spring and early summer. For the second brood, the female may build her new nest on top of the first or she may choose an entirely new site.

Construction Materials

Offering birds nesting materials is easy, low-cost, and fun—these tidbits will be gathered both by birds using your birdhouse and by those that build nests in trees. It's a great activity to do with kids, who can then watch the birds fly back and forth with their treasure. Do be sure to warn children, however, not to

Yarn	Rabbit or dog fur
Twine	Horsehair
Bakery string	Twigs
Old feathers	Evergreen needles
Goose or duck down	Dried grass

approach a nest site. The birds will be disturbed and may abandon the site, and territorial birds may try to defend their nests or fledglings by swooping at kids' heads.

Here you'll find a list of some favorite nesting materials. You can drape them from trees, pile them on old stumps, or put them in mesh bags and hang them from feeders. Never include sewing thread or fishing line in your nest offerings, as the birds may get tangled up in it. Also make sure that lengths of thicker twine or string do not exceed 4 inches (10cm), for the same reason.

Opposite: Supplying your backyard birds with nesting materials is one way to keep them coming back. Many birds construct a sturdy nest of twigs and/or grasses, then line the cup with soft materials like down, fur, and bits of yarn.

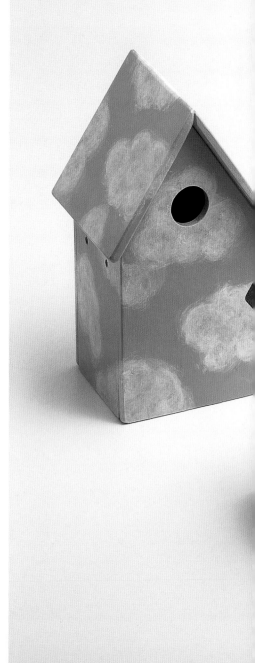

Chapter Two

Decorating Birdhouses

Before you can begin the fun of decorating your birdhouse, you'll need to prepare the surface for painting.

Follow carefully the instructions for preparing and painting your birdhouse in order to ensure maximum durability, but remember that the birdhouse will most likely need to be repainted every few seasons in any case. While some of the designs shown in this book are time-consuming to paint, none is exceptionally difficult. The sunflower and cloud designs are quite simple, and make good projects to do with the kids. Or you can let your artistic side take over and paint a design of your own creation.

Preparing the Birdhouse

1. For a smooth painting surface, apply exterior wood putty over the screws, except for the latch screw in the bottom. This needs to be left open so you can access the bottom of the house to clean the inside.

2. After the wood putty has dried, use very fine finishing sandpaper (grade #220) to sand down the excess wood putty. Use a damp soft cloth to wipe off any dust.

3. Following the manufacturer's instructions, apply two even coats of exterior latex primer to all outer surfaces of the birdhouse (be sure not to paint the inside of the entrance hole). Allow the first coat of primer to dry completely before applying the second coat. Painting in one direction from top to bottom will ensure a smoother surface. Remember to cover all surfaces completely, including the space beneath the eaves. If the painted surface is uneven after painting, use #220 grade sandpaper to smooth out the surface. You will most likely have to wait until all sides of the birdhouse are dry before you attempt to paint the bottom. Be careful to leave the latch screw unpainted, as you will need future access to this screw, and do not clog the air holes with paint. If this should happen, use a cotton swab to remove the excess paint from the air holes. Now your birdhouse is ready to decorate!

Decorating Your Birdhouse

All you will need to decorate your birdhouse are a few simple tools you probably already have at home and the paint for the decorating theme you choose. When painting the birdhouse, consider that the paint must be safe for the birds as well as durable enough for an outdoor setting. Exterior latex paint is ideal, though this type of paint tends to be sold in large quantities and can be costly if you are using a variety of colors. Many craft stores now carry small containers of exterior latex or exterior acrylic craft paints in a wide spectrum of colors, and these paints will serve your birdhouse project well. Use white and black or dark brown paints to lighten or darken your colors.

Finding all the supplies you will need and preparing your work space before you begin to paint will make decorating the birdhouse more pleasant and cleanup easier. Following is a list of items you will need, though some of the tools or supplies required depend upon the type of decorative design you choose.

- A 1¹/₂- to 2-inch paintbrush or sponge brush for applying base coats
- Several small brushes for painting fine details
- Small sea sponges for applying dappled paint in larger areas (if your design requires this)
- Cotton swabs for cleaning up any mistakes before the paint dries
- Containers for holding water and larger quantities of paint (disposable food storage containers are perfect for this)

- Container lids, wax paper, or heavy-duty aluminum foil for mixing small amounts of paint (you can also use a plastic palette from the art supply store, if you want to splurge)
- Tracing paper (if you are using one of the templates supplied in this book)
- A soft pencil (number 2 or softer)
- Low-tack drafting tape
- A burnisher, available at art supply or craft stores
- Newspaper or a drop cloth to protect your work area
- Rags or paper towels

Four of the five birdhouse designs included in this book come with templates that allow you to trace the design elements onto your birdhouse surface. If you select a design that requires one of the templates, you will have to enlarge the design to the proper size. Using a photocopier that can enlarge by percentages, input into the photocopier the percentage number marked on the bottom of the template page you are using and copy the page.

After you have enlarged your template pieces, you will create tracings from them. To do this, lay a sheet of tracing paper over the template and secure it with low-tack drafting tape. With the pencil, trace the template onto the paper, making sure all your lines are fairly dark and heavy. Once you have traced the entire template, remove the tape. Cut the individual pieces of the tracing paper down to a manageable size (but be sure not to cut across any of the pencil lines you have made).

You are now ready to transfer the design onto the birdhouse. Depending on the design, you may need to transfer different parts of the design at different stages of painting. Using the photograph of the birdhouse you chose as a guide, position the piece of tracing paper face down in place on the birdhouse surface and attach it with low-tack tape. With the burnisher, gently rub across the lines of the tracing. After you have finished rubbing across all the lines on the design, carefully remove the tape and tracing paper. You should now have guidelines to follow as you paint your design. If there are areas of the design that did not transfer as you burnished, take your pencil and fill them in freehand.

Note that some designs will require you to apply additional tracings over layers of paint. It is important to make sure that the paint is completely dry before you apply the transfer. If you accidentally remove some paint as you trace over a painted area, go back and touch up as needed. You may also find that you begin to lose your traced line as layers of paint are applied. Pencil in additional lines to guide your painting as necessary.

Sunflower Birdhouse

This cheery birdhouse calls to mind a field of sunflowers floating across a brilliant blue sky. It is relatively simple to paint, and is perfect for the novice crafter. It's important to let each application of paint dry completely before beginning the next step.

PAINT COLORS USED IN THIS DESIGN:

Bright blue

Bright yellow

Medium yellow

Dark brown

White (for lightening other paint colors, to create light and medium shades)

• Paint the entire birdhouse bright blue using a 1½- to 2-inch paintbrush or sponge brush and working from top to bottom. Remember to paint under the eaves. You may need to apply a second coat to ensure complete and even coverage.

• Attach the tracing to the roof and burnish on the sunflowers, following the general

directions for transferring designs given on pages 27–28. Remove the tracing and, using a soft pencil, fill in any lines that have not been transferred clearly. After burnishing the design onto both sides of the roof, continue freehand with a soft pencil, drawing the lines of the flower petals under the eaves.

• Trace all four walls of the birdhouse in the same fashion as the roof, remembering to continue the flower petals from the sides onto the eaves of the birdhouse. Once you have finished burnishing all the sunflowers and penciling in faint lines, you are ready to begin painting the flowers.

• You will only need to purchase two shades of yellow paint for the flowers: bright yellow and medium yellow. From these two yellows, you will create additional shades. Add a little light brown to each shade of yellow to create additional colors for the background petals. Add a little white paint to each of the two yellows to create paler shades.

• Choose a flower at random and paint the top layer of petals using one of the yellow shades (but don't use the yellows mixed with the light brown paint). Repeat coats to ensure full coverage. If the flower has back petals, paint these yellow mixed with light brown. Paint each flower in the design one of the different yellows, mixing the colors up across the birdhouse.

• After you have finished painting all the flower petals, paint the center of each sunflower dark brown. You may need to apply two coats to ensure complete coverage. Dip a brush into a lighter brown paint, using just enough paint so that when you bounce the brush on the surface you create a stippling effect. Stipple the light brown randomly onto all of the centers of the sunflowers, then repeat the process with an even lighter brown color so that each center is mottled.

Enlarge all designs by 141%

A Country Cottage

While this charming thatched cottage looks quite elaborate and takes a lot of time to complete, it is not difficult to paint using the templates provided. Remember to let each application of paint dry completely before beginning the next step.

PAINT COLORS USED IN THIS DESIGN:

Yellow ochre

Dark brown

White (for lightening other paint colors, to create light and medium shades)

Red (to add to brown, to create reddish brown)

Beige or ivory

Dark gray

Black

Deep blue

Gold

Rose pink

Dark green

THE ROOF:

• Using a 1¹/₂- to 2-inch paintbrush or sponge brush, paint the roof yellow ochre from top to bottom. Remember to paint under the eaves. You may need to apply a second coat to ensure complete and even coverage.

• Attach the tracing to the roof and burnish on the thatch design, following the general directions for transferring designs given on pages 27–28. Remove the tracing paper and use a soft pencil to fill in any faint or disconnected lines. After you have applied the tracing to both sides of the roof, continue the row lines under the eaves freehand, using a soft pencil.

• To create the thatched effect, use a thin brush to paint the thatching in three shades of brown, working from the top of the roof down toward the bottom edge. Work each row individually, starting with the top one, by painting layers of long, thin lines from top to bottom on each row. Paint one layer of reed lines using dark brown paint, a second layer with medium brown paint, and a third with reddish brown paint. Keep in mind that you are trying to mimic the look of dried

reeds overlapping each other, so complete surface coverage of these lines is not necessary. You want the existing yellow ochre color to show through from underneath.

• After you have built up your three brown layers, add some highlights randomly to the reeds with strokes of yellow ochre. To give definition to the rows, paint back over the lines segmenting the rows, using very dark brown. Thin the color a bit and paint a shadow just below the line of each row. Don't forget to paint the underside of the eaves.

THE WALLS:

• For the sides of the house, choose a light beige or ivory color as the foundation, and apply the paint evenly from top to bottom with a 1 1/2- to 2-inch paintbrush or sponge brush. You may need two coats for even coverage. If your primer was a light color, you may be able to skip this step.

• Attach the tracing to one side of the house and burnish the design onto the surface.

Burnish the design onto each side of the house (note that you will most likely need to reapply the design for the climbing rose and the flower beds after you have painted the window and stones). As you finish burnishing the design onto each wall, remove the tracing paper and fill in the lines as necessary, using a soft pencil.

• Paint the stones randomly, using either a light gray or a medium gray color. After all the stones are painted, mix both a very light gray and a dark gray color. Dip a small brush lightly into paint so that when you bounce it on the birdhouse surface you create a stippling effect. Stipple the light gray paint randomly onto all the stones, then repeat the process using the dark gray paint to create a mottled effect on the stones. Painting thin lines of varying shades of gray randomly on the stones will also help achieve this effect. Thin the dark gray and paint thin shadow lines around the stones.

THE TRIM:
• The trim around the door and windows and on the corners of the birdhouse is designed to resemble old timbers. Paint the timbers first with yellow ochre and then with medium brown.

• To create a wood grain effect, paint thin lines of varied length randomly along the timbers, using a light brown color. Using dark brown, continue painting random lines to replicate a wood grain. You may also wish to paint a few lines in a dark yellow ochre color to create more diversity in the grain. Paint each section of wood separately, so that it has the look of individual timbers. When you have finished painting the wood grain, outline each timber with a very dark brown paint. Where the wood pieces meet each other on the corners of the house, paint small black dots to resemble nails.

THE WINDOWS AND DOOR:
• The door and shutters should look like painted wood that has weathered a bit. To achieve this effect, first paint these areas with a deep blue color; two coats maybe needed for complete coverage.

• The same technique used to paint wood grain into the timbers is applied here: darken the blue paint a bit with very dark brown paint, and use this to paint the wood grain. Medium brown paint applied with short, quick brushstrokes may be used sparingly to create the weathered areas. Since this is intended to look like painted wood, it's not necessary to paint a lot of graining. Outline the planks and the windowpanes with a very dark, almost black paint. This will give definition to the individual pieces of painted wood.

• Paint the window's glass panes with two coats of a very light blue color. Create highlights in the glass panels with fine vertical strokes of white paint. Paint the doorknob gold and outline it in black.

THE CLIMBING ROSE AND FLOWER BEDS:
• If necessary, re-burnish the design for the climbing rose and the low-growing flowers at the base of the house. Begin painting the climbing rose by painting in the branches with medium brown paint. Highlight the branches here and there with light brown paint and again with a darker brown paint. This will give some dimension to the branches.

• Randomly paint clusters of three to six small circles all over the branches with a rose pink color, concentrating the clusters toward the tips of the branches. Mix some white paint with the rose pink to create a very light pink for highlighting. Paint very thin swirls within each circle to create the look of petals on a rose. Paint leaves in clusters of five around the clusters of roses, alternating light green paint with medium green for contrast.

• For the flower beds around the base of the house, paint the leaves first. Cover the mounds with leaves stroked on with medium green paint, covering the entire area designated. Here and there on the mounds, create highlights by stroking on lighter green leaves. The same can be done with dark green to create depth. Paint the flowers of some mounds by dabbing on white paint in clusters. Paint light pink flowers on alternate mounds.

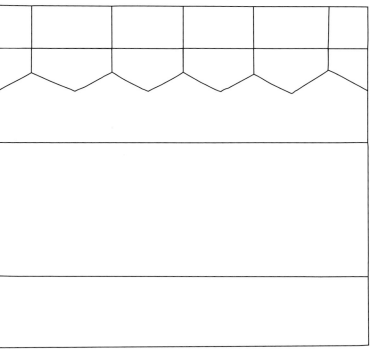

Enlarge all designs by 141%

The Barn

This birdhouse design recalls the country barns of yesteryear, with their shingles silvered with age and their traditional red paint weathered by decades of use. As you decorate the birdhouse, make sure to allow each paint application to dry before you begin the next step.

PAINT COLORS USED IN THIS DESIGN:

Dark gray

White (to add to other colors to lighten them)

Reddish brown

Dark brown

Black

Deep red

THE ROOF:

• Paint the entire roof medium gray using a 1¹/₂- to 2-inch paintbrush or sponge brush and working from top to bottom. Remember to paint under the eaves. You may need to apply a second coat to ensure complete and even coverage.

• Attach the tracing to the roof with low-tack tape and burnish on the shingles, following the general directions for transferring designs given on pages 27–28. Remove the tracing paper and, using a soft pencil, fill in any lines that did not transfer clearly. After the design has been transferred to both sides of the roof, use a soft pencil to complete the lines of the individual shingles underneath the eaves.

• To create the split-shingle effect, use a fine brush to paint long, thin lines on each shingle, starting with the top row and working each shingle individually. Work from the top of the roof down toward the bottom edge. Paint the fist layer of graining lines light gray, choosing shingles at random across the roof. Then paint fine graining lines on the rest of the shingles using a medium gray color. Use reddish brown to paint a layer of lines on all the shingles, then repeat this process using dark gray.

After you have built up your layers, add highlights to the shingles with strokes of light gray, and alternate these with random strokes of very dark brown to gain depth and definition. Keep in mind that you are emulating a split-wood grain, so complete surface coverage is not necessary: you want the existing colors to show through.

• To define the edges of the shingles, outline them using black paint. Thin the color a bit and paint a shadow just below the bottom edge of each shingle. Remember to paint the design under the eaves, too.

THE WALLS:

• Paint all four walls of the birdhouse deep red, giving the house two coats for complete coverage and working from top to bottom.

• Attach the tracing to one side of the house and burnish the design onto the house. Remove the tracing paper and fill in the lines where needed with a soft pencil.

• Using a very thin brush, outline the burnished design with black paint. Carefully fill in the wood trim for the windows and doors with white paint. Next, paint the outside edges of the birdhouse white.

• If you have accidentally painted over some of your black outlines, go back and touch up as necessary.

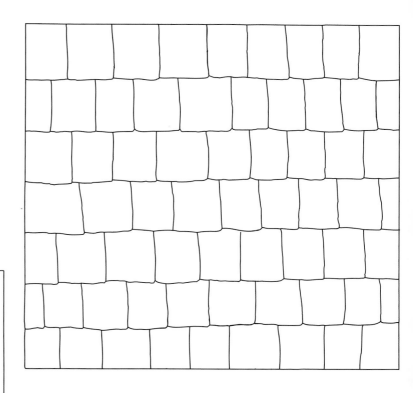

Enlarge all designs by 141%

Clouds in the Sky Birdhouse

"Clouds in the Sky" is the simplest design in this book, and should take only an hour or two to complete. Even children can participate, as long as you choose nontoxic paints and thinners. Remember to let each application of paint dry completely before beginning the next.

PAINT COLORS USED IN THIS DESIGN:

Sky blue

Cobalt

White

Light gray (optional)

• Paint the entire birdhouse sky blue using a 1¹/₂- to 2-inch paintbrush or sponge brush and working from top to bottom. Remember to paint under the eaves. You may need to apply a second coat to ensure complete coverage.

• Mix a very small amount of cobalt blue paint into the sky blue paint, to darken it just a bit. Take a small sea sponge and moisten it with water, then squeeze out all excess water. Dip the sponge into the darkened sky blue paint, and dab the paint randomly onto the birdhouse. Working quickly, lightly rub the paint into the surface with a soft rag to create some depth in the sky.

• To make the clouds, take a small sea sponge and moisten it with water, squeezing out any excess water. Dip the sponge into white paint that has been thinned with either water or with a thinner suggested by the manufacturer. Squeeze out any excess paint, then dab the sponge onto the surface of the birdhouse, using a clockwise circular motion. The result should be a swirl of white with sky blue still showing through in places. You may want to practice the technique first on some scrap paper.

Scatter the clouds in a carefree way across the surfaces of the birdhouse, remembering to continue some of the clouds underneath the eaves. Cluster some overlapping swirls to create billowy clouds.

• If you want to add some depth to the clouds, take another small sea sponge and moisten it with water, squeezing out any excess. Dip the sponge into very light gray paint that has been thinned and squeeze out any excess paint. Dab the sponge lightly over the tops of the white areas of the clouds, applying the paint sparingly; only small amounts of dappled gray should appear on the tops of the clouds. This will add dimension. If the clouds should become too dense with layers of white and gray paint, randomly dab sky blue paint throughout the clouds to create a sense of transparency.

Black Forest Birdhouse

This birdhouse design was inspired by the cottages found in fairy tales, and is intended to look like a little house made completely of wood. Like the Country Cottage, this birdhouse design is time-consuming to execute but is not difficult to paint if you follow the directions and use the templates provided. Allow each application of paint to dry completely before beginning the next step.

PAINT COLORS USED IN THIS DESIGN:

Yellow ochre

Dark brown

White (for lightening other paint colors, to create light and medium shades)

Red (also used to create reddish brown)

Black

Blue

Yellow

Gold

THE ROOF:

- Paint the entire roof yellow ochre using a 1½- to 2-inch paintbrush or sponge brush and working from top to bottom. Remember to paint under the eaves. You may need to apply a second coat to ensure complete and even coverage.

- Attach the tracing to the roof with low-tack tape and burnish on the shingles and border design, following the general directions for transferring designs given on pages 27–28. You may need to re-burnish the wood borders of the birdhouse after you have painted the shingles. Remove the tracing paper and use a soft pencil to fill in any lines that were not transferred clearly. After applying the design to both sides of the roof, draw the cutout designs under the eaves, using a soft pencil.

- Both the shingles and the borders will be painted to mimic wood. The split-shingle effect is created by using a thin brush and working from the top of the roof down toward the bottom edge. Starting with the top row, work each shingle individually, painting layers of long thin lines from top to bottom. Paint the first layer light brown, applying thin lines of paint randomly across the roof on various shingles. Paint the remaining shingles with thin lines in a medium brown color. Use reddish brown paint to paint a layer of lines on all of the shingles; repeat this process with a dark brown color, again applying the lines to all of the shingles. Keep in mind that you are copying the look of a split wood grain, so complete surface coverage is not necessary: you want the existing colors to show through from underneath.

- After you have built up the layers, randomly add highlights to the shingles with strokes of yellow ochre. Alternate with very dark brown to gain some depth and definition. To bring definition to the outlines of the shingles, paint back over the lines with black. Thin the color a bit and paint a shadow just beneath the lower edge of each shingle.

• The border trim on the roof should be painted using the same technique used for the shingles, but using medium brown for all of the pieces. Remember to paint underneath the eaves. After you have achieved the desired wood grain effect, paint the sides of the roof border lightly with yellow ochre, letting some of the wood grain show through in areas. For the top border on the roof, paint lightly over the graining with red (you may wish to thin the red paint). Again, allow the wood grain to show through. If too much area is covered, stroke randomly with brown paint.

• Attach the tracing paper again and burnish on the cutout design for the borders. Remove the tracing paper and fill in the cutout design using black paint. Remember to paint the design under the eaves.

THE WALLS:

• All four walls of the birdhouse should be painted with two coats of yellow ochre paint. Paint from top to bottom to ensure even coverage. Attach the tracing to one side of the house and burnish the design onto the house. Burnish on the design for each wall in turn, but note that you will probably have to burnish again the designs that decorate the shutters, window boxes, or wood borders of the birdhouse after you have painted in their wood grain. Remove the tracing paper and fill in any lines as needed using a soft pencil.

• Paint the horizontal wood planks on each side, using a medium brown color. To create a wood grain effect, paint thin, light brown lines of varying length randomly along the planks. Paint each section of wood separately, so that it has the look of individual planks. Repeat the process of applying random lines, using first dark brown paint and then reddish brown. You may also wish to paint a few lines in dark yellow ochre and dark brown to create more diversity in the grain. Outline the wood pieces with a very dark brown paint. Thin the color a bit and paint a shadow just below the line of each wooden plank and in between them.

HOUSE DETAILS:

• The trim, shutters, window boxes, door, and border designs repeat the same wood grain painting technique as the border designs on the roof, however the trim around the windows will not feature the additional bright-colored paint added to it. After you have achieved the desired wood grain effect on these elements, apply blue paint over the graining on the window boxes and shutters, and red paint over the corner border designs of the birdhouse sides. Use yellow paint to brighten the border design around the door. Remember to let the wood grain show through. If too much area is covered, stroke randomly with brown paint.

• Attach the tracing paper again and burnish on the cutout design for the shutters, window boxes, and borders. Remove the tracing paper and fill in the cutout design with black paint.

• The window's glass panes should be painted with two coats of a very light blue color. Attach the tracing paper again and burnish on the cutout design for the windowpanes. Remove the tracing paper and outline these designs with black paint; then create highlights in the glass panes with fine vertical strokes of white paint.

• Paint the wood panels of the door using the same technique as for the wood planks of the walls, but with much less color. First apply a layer of light brown lines, then a layer of medium brown. Outline each plank with dark brown paint and paint the iron hardware across the door black. Finally, paint the doorknob gold and outline it in black.

Enlarge all designs by 141%

Chapter Three

Attracting Birds to Your Yard

ortunately for backyard birders, winged creatures'
needs are not difficult to meet. In fact, they require

the same basic necessities that humans need to thrive:

food, water, and shelter. But these three elements

must not only be accessible, they must be arranged in

a way that makes the birds feel safe and secure. Your

backyard may already have many of the elements you

need to welcome birds. If it doesn't, making space for

a few of the birds' simple requirements is generally an

easy and rewarding task.

*Right: Simple yet elegant, this classic pedestal birdbath invites birds to drink
and bathe. The accompanying planting is exquisite, but is safest for birds if
the neighborhood is free of roaming cats. Otherwise, leave space around the
bath so that birds have warning of approaching predators.*

Survey Your Garden

Before hanging your birdhouse or buying your first sunflower seed, take a good look at your yard to assess its bird-friendliness. Sometimes the very areas you consider problems are the foundation of a bird haven. Perhaps there's a dead tree in that little grove at the back of your lot, or maybe there's a stand of tall, fence-hugging grasses that you've been meaning to mow down. Before you clean up your yard, remember that an overly manicured landscape is not a good place for birds to live and raise families.

Often, gardening for the birds is a matter of unlearning some of our long-honored gardening traditions. Heavily pruned trees, tightly sheared shrubs, carpets of short-cut grass, isolated island beds of exotic annuals, and stiff, hybridized tea roses regularly misted with chemical pesticides combine to make a bird's worst nightmare. Birds have always embraced the idea of the natural garden, and modern homeowners are now catching up. Let nature be your guide

Below: Tickseed sunflowers are magnets for butterflies as well as for small birds, as these golden, daisylike flowers supply rich nectar and plentiful seeds.

Opposite: Tall flowers and grasses growing up around a fence create a safe corridor that birds can use to travel about the yard. When autumn arrives, the dried stalks and seedheads should be left in place—they'll continue to offer cover and will provide seeds for hungry birds.

when you are planning a bird-friendly garden—remember that Mother Nature has protected her bird species for millennia. Shady woodlands, wildflower-dotted meadows, dry deserts punctuated by prickly cactus, and boggy stands of cattails all harbor happy birds. Choosing a garden style that suits your region and your garden space is much easier than working against nature. A mix of plants in varied forms, textures, and sizes is the most effective way to be sure birds are secure.

But it's not enough to plant a bird-attracting shrub and expect that birds will begin to frequent your yard. A bird out in the open is a bird vulnerable to predators. To feel comfortable, birds need a variety of places where they can perch safely and they need secure avenues of cover that they can use to move about the yard. Planting plenty of trees, shrubs, tall grasses, and wildflowers at different heights and in natural-looking drifts, and using these plants to help integrate features such as feeders and birdbaths, gives the birds places to hide in the event that a hawk or a cat happens along.

When you survey your yard, take a pad of paper with you and jot down all the features you have that you want to keep. Then, as you read through this book and research the elements you'd like to add, make a separate column for your wish list. Many gardeners find it helpful to draw a garden plan on a piece of graph paper. This way, you will be able to plan with the garden's scale in mind, and can allow for the eventual size of plants, the appropriate distances of nest boxes, and so on.

Don't panic if the work and expense of creating your ideal bird-lover's garden seems overwhelming at first. Remember that almost all gardens are works in progress, and your bird-lover's garden will likely be no different, evolving over time as you see what works best for you and

your feathered visitors. You can add a plant or a bird-friendly element here and there, as you have time and money. The birds will appreciate even a modest effort, and with a plan in hand, you will be working efficiently toward your ultimate goal.

Above: A garden filled with a variety of fruiting, flowering, and foliage plants will provide the food and cover that backyard birds crave.

Above: White-breasted nuthatches typically feed head down, searching the tree trunk for insects, so they appreciate a yard with plenty of mature trees. They'll also eat beechnuts, acorns, and sunflower seeds.

Consider Planting for the Birds

Planting species native to your region is a sure way to attract birds. Birds have evolved over millennia to expect certain plants in certain areas, and they have long-developed tastes for the seeds, fruits, and nectars native to the region where they are living. This is not to say that they don't appreciate other types of plants and supplemental feeding, particularly in harsh weather, but generally birds' diets have been well established by native availability over many, many thousands of years.

A benefit of landscaping with native plants is that they are generally easy to grow because they are adapted for the conditions in your region. They'll need less attention from you, so you'll have more time to enjoy your birds and your garden.

Growing native plants also lends your garden a strong sense of regional character and helps to integrate your yard into the larger landscape. Visiting local parks and botanical gardens will give you an appreciation of the plants that grow well in your part of the country, and local garden clubs and horticultural societies are usually happy to offer advice.

Many native species have traits, such as rich fragrance or an abundance of nectar, that may have been hybridized out of modern cultivars. If you are planning on purchasing a cultivated variety of a plant (and in many cases you may want certain new cultivars for their ornamental value, increased hardiness, or resistance to pests or diseases), be sure to ask the nursery if the plant has retained its bird-attracting qualities. If the improved cultivar doesn't possess the traits birds are drawn to, you'll need to consider whether you want to go ahead and plant the native species (though it may be more subtle in its charms or more prone to disease) or choose a different plant altogether.

Above: Native to North America, purple coneflowers are particular favorites of goldfinches and sparrows, who prize the seeds.

Above: Blueberries are among birds' favorite foods. These shrubs are very versatile, as they feature attractive spring flowers, delicious fruit, and lovely autumn color. They are also easy to grow, requiring only soil that is moist, fertile, and slightly acidic.

Give a Year-Round Banquet

Birds benefit from a healthy selection of their favorite foods growing in the garden, as well as from supplemental offerings at bird feeders, especially in the depth of winter. Fruiting trees and shrubs, together with grasses and flowers that bear snack-worthy seeds, are ideal choices for your bird haven. Planning for year-round provisions helps keep the birds happy, healthy, and flocking to your garden. Different birds have different food preferences, and learning the favorite treats of the birds you want to attract will give you greater success in drawing them.

A garden design that includes a variety of fruiting plants that bear in succession throughout the year ensures a good turnout of birds. Spring and summer are easy times for birds, as nature is awash with insects and fresh fruits. Wild strawberries are excellent choices for groundcovers, and their fruit is adored by birds. Any fruit tree is sure to be a success—try cherry, apricot, or peach trees. Berry bushes, too, make perfect natural bird feeders, with raspberries, elderberries, and blueberries leading the pack in terms of bird favorites. Grapes will also be deeply appreciated.

Viburnums and sumacs take over the duties in autumn, and birds flock to their shining fruits. In winter, feathered visitors are drawn to the fruits of the holly, pyracantha, and cotoneaster. It is in the winter season that birds rely most on their human friends. Feeders filled with nutritious seeds and suet help keep the birds that have stuck around healthy 'til spring.

Above: About 30 percent of the black-capped chickadee's diet consists of fruits like winterberry and viburnum and the seeds of conifers like pine and hemlock. It also eats many insect pests, such as aphids and snails, which makes the chickadee a welcome visitor to the garden.

Hummingbirds, those buzzing, glittering gems of the bird world, have their own special needs, and feed primarily on insects and flower nectar. Hummers are attracted by bright flowers, particularly red and orange, and prefer blooms in tubular shapes, like those of the trumpet vine.

Setting the Table

A selection of food-producing trees, flowers, and shrubs growing in the landscape is best for the birds, but there may be times you'll want to supplement your garden's offerings with seeds or other

Above: The thistle seed provided in this feeder is a sure-fire draw: here, it has attracted a bevy of birds, including a house finch, American goldfinches, and an indigo bunting.

food set out in bird feeders. Filling your feeders will ensure that seed-loving birds visit often and are cared for through winter or when times are hard. Wild bird seed mixes are widely available, and will generally include several types of sunflowers, millet, buckwheat, and a tiny seed called canary seed. While some birds are perfectly happy with this mix, others are more choosy, and will discard the seeds they don't like, scattering them on the ground about the feeder.

Some gardeners stop feeding birds when winter is over and plants begin providing enough nutrition (and, indeed, many birds lose interest in store-bought seed when better pickin's come along), while other bird lovers continue to set out treats all year long. Whatever you choose to do, there are a few bird-feeding dos and don'ts that you should be aware of. In the following section, you'll learn which feeders are best for your needs and where to put your feeder so that birds can eat safely.

To get the most joy out of your bird feeder, site it where you'll be able to watch the birds easily. Depending on your climate and your habits, this might mean placing your feeder in view of a window, where you can relax in comfort and watch the antics of your feathered visitors. Or you might choose to

Above: Suet, a hard fat found in beef and mutton, is a favorite of birds. The northern flicker and Carolina chickadee visiting this feeder ignore the traditional seed mix in favor of the fat-rich treat.

site your feeder where you can enjoy it from a favorite lawn chair, outdoors and at one with the garden.

The ideal situation is to set up several feeders, which will attract an array of different birds. In addition to giving you more opportunities for good viewing, installing a couple of feeders means that you can provide for more birds. When only one feeder is available, the larger, more aggressive birds may outcompete the smaller, more timid ones for the much-desired food. If other feeders are present and there is enough food to go around, the more bashful birds can visit without being chased by the bullies.

Which Food for Which Bird?

Birds have their own favorite foods, which will have them flocking to your feeders. Following is a chart of some of these preferred treats and the birds they'll attract.

Treat	Bird Attracted
Peanut butter and chopped nut meats	Blue jay, cardinal, catbird, chickadee, finch, grosbeak, nuthatch, titmouse, woodpecker, sparrow
Suet	Brown creeper, chickadee, blue jay, golden- and ruby crowned kinglet, flicker, red- and white-breasted nuthatch, red-winged blackbird, titmouse, woodpecker
Sunflower seeds	Blue jay, cardinal, chickadee, crossbill, goldfinch, evening grosbeak, mourning dove, purple finch, siskin, white-crowned sparrow, titmouse
Small mixed seed	Brown thrasher, cardinal, catbird, American goldfinch, hermit thrush, horned lark, house finch, junco, mourning dove, pine siskin, evening and pine grosbeak, purple finch, redwing, scrub jay, snow bunting, sparrow, titmouse
Large seed (kernel corn, oats, rye, wheat, etc.)	Blue grosbeak, blue jay, meadowlark, mourning dove, pheasant, quail, ruffed grouse, woodpecker
Chopped fruit (apple, apricot, banana, blueberry, cherry, cranberry, fig, peach, raisin, strawberry, etc.)	Baltimore oriole, bluebird, catbird, cedar waxwing, hermit thrush, mockingbird, myrtle warbler, robin, thrasher, woodpecker

You might choose cracked corn, which tends to draw ground-feeding bird. Thistle seed (also sold as niger seed) is relatively expensive, but is favored by the much-sought-after goldfinches. Because this seed is fine, you'll need to use a special thistle seed feeder. Peanuts are easy to come by, and are beloved by titmice, jays, and chickadees.

Above: An array of different feeders containing a variety of seed types—combined with a healthy number of trees and shrubs—provides the ideal feeding environment. There is enough food that the birds don't need to compete, and there are safe places to fly for cover if a cat or hawk approaches.

Note that some birds feed on the ground, and will scratch in the dust around a bird feeder for fallen seeds. These birds are particularly vulnerable to cats, so if you have cats roaming your neighborhood, make sure there are no shrubs or dense plantings that could conceal cats near your feeder. This way, ground-feeding birds will have warning if a cat approaches and will have a chance to fly to safety.

Above: A downy woodpecker relishes the offerings at a backyard feeder. These energetic birds are year-round visitors to feeders, especially where they can indulge their passion for beef suet.

Different Kinds of Feeders

There is a vast range of bird feeders on the market, from simple wooden trays to elaborate reproductions of landmark buildings. There are feeders to suit every type of bird and to catch every gardener's fancy as well. Some are highly ornamental, while others' virtues are chiefly functional. All feeders do have one thing in common, however: all require care and attention from the gardener. Wet seed soon becomes spoiled with mold, while an unstocked feeder disappoints birds, who may stop visiting. An even bigger problem faces those who use feeders that are fully open to the birds, for here bird feces can collect, leading to a proliferation of bacteria.

A well-designed feeder and careful maintenance will help solve many of these problems. Following is a description of the main types of feeders and the specific advantages and disadvantages of each. All feeders should be checked daily to be certain that clean, dry food is available. Feeders should regularly be emptied of their contents and cleaned with a 10 percent bleach solution to disinfect them.

Which Feeder for Which Bird?

In addition to having their preferred foods, some birds have favorite types of feeders. This chart will help you decide which feeder option is most likely to attract the types of birds you'd like to have in your backyard.

Feeder Type	Birds Attracted
Tube feeder	American goldfinch, black-capped chickadee, house finch, linnet, tufted titmouse, goldfinch, pine siskin, purple finch, sparrow, and other small seed eaters
Hopper feeder	Blue jay, cardinal, evening grosbeak, house finch, jay, mourning dove, pine siskin, purple finch
Platform feeder (used for fruit and suet in addition to seed)	Bunting, cardinal, catbird, chickadee, flicker, goldfinch, jay, junco, mockingbird, Northern oriole, nuthatch, pine siskin, red-winged blackbird, sapsucker, scarlet tanager, sparrow, thrush, towhee, tufted titmouse, woodpecker
Hummingbird feeder	Hummingbird, Northern oriole, nuthatch, sparrow, tanager, thrush, titmouse, warbler
Suet feeder	Flicker, nuthatch, sapsucker, woodpecker

Above: This platform feeder features a roof, which helps keep seed dry in inclement weather. Platform feeders are highly democratic, and may attract birds you don't wish to entertain, like these European starlings, who outcompete native birds for limited resources.

PLATFORM FEEDERS

Platform feeders are simply flat trays with a slightly raised edge, which prevents seed from spilling over the side or blowing away. This type of feeder is highly visible to birds, and will begin attracting them right away. Remember that a larger tray will attract more birds without fear of crowding. You can install a platform feeder at any number of heights—a feeder set only a few inches above the earth will be a magnet for ground-feeding birds. Other birds will be nervous feeding on the ground, and will be happier with a platform installed a few feet above the grass.

Platform feeders can be stocked with any type of seed or seed mix, as well as with fruit or suet. Some gardeners even set mealworms out on platform feeders to attract insect-eating birds.

The main disadvantage of platform feeders is that they are open to the sky, and thus the seed gets wet when it rains. Make sure your platform feeders feature plenty of drainage holes, and clean them thoroughly whenever they get wet, as damp, moldy seed will be rejected by the birds.

HOPPER FEEDERS

This type of feeder has a roof, a decided advantage in keeping foods dry and free from birds' bodily wastes and other debris. The sides are usually made of clear plastic, but may be constructed of some other material, such as wood. The seeds fall down through a small gap between the walls and the feeder's floor, and the birds reach the food through this opening.

Above: Social house finches are a common sight at backyard feeders, and they are not choosy about their diet. They'll eat almost any type of birdseed offered, and will often help themselves at nectar, fruit, and suet feeders as well.

Hopper feeders that feature attached perches are best, since the birds will not be able to soil the seed with droppings. Wide troughs below the gap mean that there will be a need for frequent cleanings, which can prove tiresome, especially of your feeder is not conveniently located. You'll also want to be sure that the gap between walls and floors is narrow, or small birds may go in through the opening and be trapped. To minimize these problems, check the feeder carefully before you buy.

Above: A pair of American goldfinches dines at a tube feeder filled with their favorite thistle seeds.

TUBE FEEDERS

Tube feeders are generally made of plastic, and, like hopper feeders, have openings through which the birds can get at seed. The dining birds rest on perches attached near the openings, so the food will not become contaminated with bird feces. If you look for a model with a tight-fitting waterproof lid, the seed should remain dry and fresh.

Tube feeders are popular with certain birds, such as titmice, siskins, and finches. This type of feeder may not attract as many birds, but it does protect seed from rainstorms.

FRUIT FEEDERS

Fruit feeders are mainly intended to attract orioles, and chiefly consist of a short spike upon which a half an orange (or another piece of fruit) may be impaled. The fancier models may have roofs and perches, but the birds don't require this. You can simply spear a fruit piece at the end of a bare tree branch, or construct a simple fruit feeder from a long nail driven through a piece of wood. Do be sure to affix the feeder at a height where the nail will not injure children or anyone else who might happen by.

SUET FEEDERS

Suet is almost always provided in a special cage-style feeder, or occasionally in plastic mesh bags, because it is such a treat that birds will abscond with it and carry it away to a tree where they can eat it out of view. The cage protects the suet from thievery by just one bird, allowing a multitude to enjoy the offering. Both suet cages and cakes of commercially prepared suet are available from specialty stores and mail-order sources.

NECTAR FEEDERS

Hummingbird feeders are sure to attract these delightful little birds to your outdoor space. If possible, choose a bright red one with several flower-shaped feeding ports. If you can't find one of this design, do try to make sure that it has the bright red coloring so attractive to these diminutive birds. A good hummingbird feeder will have a "bee guard," a small screen that covers the port and keeps bees and wasps out of the nectar, but allows hummers' bills to get at the concoction. You'll want to make sure that the feeder you buy is easy to clean, as the instant nectar or sugar water you use to fill the feeder is subject to mold, which is bad for the hummingbirds. Clean the feeder often, and refill it regularly.

Above: Mesh keeps the suet cake intact so that it can be enjoyed by all the birds, though this red-breasted nuthatch appears to have designs on the cherished foodstuff.

Hand-Feeding Birds

There is some controversy about whether wild birds should become accustomed to direct contact with people. Clearly, becoming habituated to humans means that some birds may put themselves at risk by approaching people who do not have their best interests at heart. Yet many people enjoy trying to get birds to feed from their hands, and indeed entire books have been devoted to the subject. Remember that this is a project that requires a lot of patience.

You may have noticed that birds come when you put out food. To begin getting your backyard birds to visit on cue, use a specific sound, such as a small bell, each time you put out food. Continue for several weeks.

After the birds begin to come on cue, begin sitting in the vicinity of the feeder after you ring the bell. Sit very still for about fifteen minutes each time, gradually moving your chair closer to the food source.

Once the birds have become used to your presence, empty most of the food tray, leaving some seed in one section. Put some food in your hand and place your hand, opened flat, near the food tray. (Note that some people have had success by first placing an empty glove with food in the palm near the feeder tray.) You must be extremely still and quiet. Do not swallow—swallowing makes the bird think of you as a predator. Do not look at birds that arrive.

Speak in a gentle conversational voice. When a bird finally lands on your hand to feed, do not move and do not attempt to touch the bird. Some bird species are more readily accepting of hand feeding than others. Among these are chickadees, titmice, jays, and, of course, pigeons.

Opposite: With patience, you can coax a Carolina chickadee to eat from your hand.

Don't Forget the H$_2$O

Like all living things, birds need water. A ready supply of fresh water will soon register with birds in your area, and they'll remember the source when they need it. Insect- and seed-eaters usually require more drinking water than birds that eat fruit, but whatever their diet, all birds will appreciate a good water source. Remember that water is especially important to birds in times of drought or in the winter, when available water is far less plentiful.

While birds can find often find water to drink from a variety of natural sources, such as puddles and dew on leaves, there isn't always enough to bathe in, so they'll be delighted to find a full birdbath in your garden. Insect-eating species generally won't visit a feeder, so supplying water will draw birds you may not otherwise have an opportunity to see. Especially in dry regions such as the desert Southwest, birds will be reliably attracted by the promise of ample fresh water.

Bathing keeps feathers in good condition, and is necessary to the health of a bird. By soaking, splashing, and shaking themselves, then preening, birds rid themselves of dirt and dust. Birds need their feathers to fly, but also to keep themselves warm in winter and cool in summer.

Below: Insect-eaters like this hungry house wren, whose diet is 97 percent insects, won't flock to your backyard feeders, so to get a better look at these birds consider installing a birdbath.

Integrate a birdbath or another small water feature into your garden, and you'll find a variety of visitors there daily. Do consider that birds are vulnerable when bathing: the neighborhood cat or a passing hawk can swoop in and catch a bird at the moment when it is thoroughly waterlogged and unable to fly very far. Placing your birdbath beneath a tree but several yards away from concealing shrubs will shield songbirds from the overhead gaze of a predatory bird and give them an emergency perch, but will prevent a cat from sneaking up unannounced.

CHOOSING THE RIGHT BATH

There are scores of different types of birdbaths available today, and you are certain to find one that suits your taste and your garden's mood. Birdbaths can be found in ceramic, terra-cotta, cast stone or concrete, or plastic, and each of these materials has its advantages and disadvantages. Ceramic, terra-cotta, and stone or concrete are the most ornamental but these may freeze and crack during cold winter weather unless the water inside is kept constantly heated with an electric birdbath heater. Plastic is unlikely to break from freezing (though it sometimes becomes brittle if left exposed for long periods of time), and has the added bonus of being lightweight, but tends to be less attractive.

Opposite: Birdbaths are available in a range of shapes, sizes, colors, and materials. This hanging glazed terra-cotta example is an interesting garden ornament as well as a functional birdbath. If you choose a glazed bath, do make sure that the bottom is not too slippery.

The traditional shallow basin set atop a pedestal is a good choice for a birdbath, but you needn't limit yourself to this design. Any shallow dish will work just fine—the clay saucers intended for use beneath planters make superb birdbaths. You do need to make sure that the

Above: This handsome pedestal birdbath, complete with a sculptured bird, is well positioned for a garden that might harbor predators. Slabs of slate assure that bathing birds will be able to see a cat approach across the open ground, allowing the birds time to escape.

bottom surface of the bath is not too slippery. If you are concerned that it's too slick, the problem can be easily remedied. Simply set a flat, rough stone on the bottom to give the birds better footing.

Many birds adapted for land living avoid deep water, as they can drown quite easily. Their small, twig-like feet are not designed for swimming, so they tend to gravitate to shallow puddles or brooks. The ideal birdbath will have graduated depths, with the water only about half an inch (1.3cm) deep at the edges and no more than three inches (7.7cm) deep at its greatest depth. This way, both small and larger birds will be able to bathe comfortably.

For a more natural-looking bath, you might choose a hollowed stone set on the ground. This sort of feature is perfect for woodland spaces or for wilderness-inspired gardens.

Winter Bathing

Birds like to bathe even in winter, and you can draw winged visitors to your garden in the cold weather by installing an electric heater in your birdbath. These heaters are widely available at pet-supply stores and through specialty catalogs, and are incredibly easy to use. In most cases, you need only set the heater in the bath and plug it in. If your outdoor electrical outlet is far from your birdbath, you'll need to invest in a sturdy outdoor extension cord. Alternatively, you could move your bath a bit closer to the house for the winter months.

Above: Birdbath heaters—which you can purchase inexpensively through mail-order catalogs or in pet stores— give your year-round feathered neighbors a place to bathe even in the depths of winter.

If you are not going to heat your birdbath water, be sure to empty the basin and store the birdbath indoors for the winter, unless you live in a warm climate. Many birdbath materials are susceptible to cracks and breakage through repeated freezing and thawing, and you'll want to spare yourself the expense of replacing your bath every year.

Birds will also visit and bathe in a shallow garden pool or slow-running stream, so if you have a water feature in your yard, you may not need to do much else.

A mister or dripper, available from bird supply or specialty gardening stores and catalogs, will get even more attention from the birds, who gravitate to the sound of moving water.

MAINTAINING THE BIRDBATH

Keep your birdbath pristine by cleaning it out and refilling it with fresh water every day. Birdbaths filled with dirt and debris will soon also be filled with algae and harmful bacteria, and birds know to keep away from such dangers. Make sure to site your birdbath so that routine maintenance tasks are convenient; otherwise, you'll find yourself neglecting this important step and your visitors will stop coming. Put the birdbath within easy reach of the hose and keep a small scrub brush handy. Every few weeks, you'll need to clean the bird-

Above: A Carolina chickadee perches on the edge of a birdbath. Regular refilling and proper cleaning keep birds coming back to the bath again and again.

bath with bleach or a commercial cleanser to get rid of any dirty buildup. Do be sure, before refilling the basin, that you've thoroughly rinsed off all cleanser residue. You might also try cleaning the bath with a solution of water and white vinegar—this will keep the birdbath clean and is less harsh than bleach.

Be kind to yourself, and place birdbaths at least 5 feet (1.5m) away from bird feeders. Some of our feathered friends are messy eaters, and if you position your birdbath in close proximity to food, you'll find the water full of leftovers and bird droppings, complicating your cleaning chores. Putting the birdbath within visual distance of a feeder, however, will ensure that birds notice it.

Conclusion

As you observe the birds in your yard, you'll see that their range of diet and eating habits is as wide as their other behaviors. Once you've put up your birdhouse and provided for the birds' food and water needs, you'll be in a good position to get to know the birds in your neighborhood; a field guide or a knowledgeable friend can help you identify and understand your backyard visitors. This will help you become a better backyard birder and is a rewarding pastime in and of itself.

Resources

Berry Hill Limited
75 Burwell Road
St. Thomas, Ontario
Canada N5P 3R5
800-668-3072
Birdhouses, bird feeders

Bruce Barber Bird Feeders, Inc.
4600 Jason Street
Denver, CO 80211
800-528-2794
*Handcrafted birdhouses,
bird feeders*

Duncraft
PO Box 9020
Penacook, NH 03303-9020
800-593-5656
www.duncraft.com
*Birdhouses, baths, feeders, seed
mixes and treats, and many more
bird fostering accessories*

Earthly Goods Ltd.
PO Box 614
New Albany, IN 47150
812-944-3283
*Nesting boxes, bird feeders,
grasses, wildflowers*

Gardeners Eden
PO Box 7307
San Francisco, CA 94120-7307
800-822-9600
Birdbaths, bird feeders

Lazy Hill Farm Designs
PO Box 235
Lazy Hill Road
Colerain, NC 27924
919-356-2040
Birdhouses, feeders, nesting boxes

Perky-Pet Brand
www.perkypet.com
Wild bird feeders, accessories

Wild Birds Forever
www.birdsforever.com
*Bird feeders, birdbath heaters,
binoculars, books, ornaments*

Wild Birds Unlimited
11711 N. College Ave.
Suite 146
Carmel, IN 46032-5655
800-326-4928 (store locator)
www.wbu.com
*Feeders, nesting boxes, birdbaths,
seed mixes and treats*

Photo Credits

Daybreak Imagery: ©Richard Day: pp. 5, 10, 13, 19, 23, 50–51, 53, 60, 61, 63, 72, 75, 77, 78; ©Susan Day: pp. 14, 66

Dembinsky Photo Associates: ©Jim Battles: pp. 2, 56; ©Willard Clay: p. 52; ©Sharon Cummings: pp. 11, 64; ©Dan Dempster: p. 18; ©Darrell Gulin: p. 55; ©Randall B. Henne: pp. 67, 68, 69; ©Adam Jones: p. 73; ©Ed Kanze: p. 21; ©Doug Locke: p. 57; ©Anthony Mercieca: p. 6; ©Larry Mishkar: p. 71; ©Skip Moody: pp. 7, 59; ©Rod Planck: p. 58; ©George E. Stuart: p. 16

Folio, Inc.: ©Everett C. Johnson: p. 8–9; ©Tal McBride: p. 17

Dennis Galante: pp. 3, 24–25, 28, 29, 32, 38, 43, 44

©Jerry Pavia: p. 76